FOUR BLACK REVOLUTIONARY PLAYS

(All Praises to the Black Man)

FOUR BLACK REVOLUTIONARY PLAYS

Experimental Death Unit 1
A Black Mass
Great Goodness of Life
Madheart

Amiri Baraka

With a Foreword by Lindsay Barrett

MARION BOYARS
LONDON • NEW YORK

Reprinted in 2009 by Marion Boyars Publishers Ltd,
24 Lacy Road, London, SW15 1NL
www.marionboyars.co.uk

First published in the United States in 1969 by the Bobs-Merrill Company Inc
First published in Great Britain in 1971 by Calder and Boyars Publishers Ltd

10 9 8 7 6 5 4 3

Distributed in Australia by Tower Books Pty Ltd, Unit 2, 17 Rodborough Road, Frenchs Forest, NSW 2086, Australia

A CIP catalogue record for this book is available from the British Library.
A CIP catalog record for this book is available from the Library of Congress.

ISBN 978-0-7145-3005-5

CONTENTS

FOREWORD

The most perceptive critical assessments of the work of Amiri Baraka (LeRoi Jones) in the early stages of his literary career noted that subtle, and often oblique, expressions of rebellion against middle-class values energized his aesthetic principles. At the same time a studied concentration on linguistic innovation in his early poetry established a foundation of creative insurgency as the most important functional element of his vision. An obsessive adherence to these principles in his work helped to revolutionize American poetry in the fifties and sixties. He developed and implemented a theory of poetic commitment to psychological and social reform into a body of structural expression, in which both form and content were continually revitalized by experimentation and rigorous intellectual self-examination and argument. In the process of developing his literary career, Baraka moved from being a precociously influential poet in his youth to become a profoundly influential dramatist in his maturity.

A fundamental characteristic of Baraka's creative output is that it has always retained both combative and lyrical elements through the several phases of revolt, and demonstrable change, which constantly reformed his personal socio-political perceptions. The extension into his personal life of the spirit of inner creative conflict which this aesthetic tension established in his work has been documented in the annals of American creative history of the modern era, but it is the deeply committed injection of a conscious portrayal, and analysis, of racial (and indeed 'racist') experience in American society which informs every root and branch of his creative life. The plays included in this volume are reports from the soul of this aspect of Baraka's creative experience.

Basically a poet, Baraka's political vision, as interpreted in his 'black revolutionary plays', is translated into impressionistic language by instinct rather than by analysis. This instinctive quality is to be found in abundance in the poetry of his youthful 'beatnik' period. He virtually coerced the processes of didactic revolutionary expression into service in his later creative work, however, and his ideas gained force by being translated into active drama rather than passive poetry in the mid-sixties. His work became increasingly impressionistic even as he sought to make it carry the burden of programmatic propaganda for the anti-bourgeois, and anti-racist, revolution which radical political thinkers expected to be the natural consequence of the Afro-American civil rights movement. Baraka's adherence to these values in his writing caused him to be regarded as something of an *enfant terrible* by the American theatrical establishment. His decision to move his thematic concerns towards the process of not merely influencing but actually encouraging a revolution in racial attitudes and relationships through formal dramatic expression brought several challenges to the fore not only in his creative work but also in his personal perceptions of political experience.

At the heart of these works there is a desperate sense of emotional torment. His 'revolutionary' plays, as distinct from his relatively more traditional works, emerge as cries of pain rather than as examinations of circumstance. It is worth noting though that, while the themes of these plays seemed almost predictable, especially against the background of the communal upheaval of the era in which they were written and performed (from 1964–1966), none of his works in their vein were ever purely rudimentary in form. Their deceptive simplicity disguise a profound formal evaluation of the sociological sources and the political objectives which gave them birth.

The opening play in this anthology, *Experimental Death Unit 1*, provides a clear example of how Baraka's understanding of dramatic sensationalism and surrealist symbolism were placed at the service of political protest when he made the leap from creative introspection to socio-political commentary. The primary theme of this one-act deliberation is arguably a humorous, but at the same time tragic, acknowledgement of the power of the taboos and the misconceptions surrounding interracial sexual desire. In this work both sexual desire and pornographic depravity are depicted as co-habitants of an impulsively dysfunctional urban setting. The profound sense of loss and strain which underlies this deliberately pornographic exercise drives home the poignant message that, inevitably, corrupt power generates its own destruction.

A Black Mass, the play which follows, is another matter entirely. It utilizes many of the same literary devices and creative impulses to build a vision of a people seeking truth from the viewpoint of a self-righteous myth. Baraka's reworking of this fundamentally separatist racial myth is a powerful rendition of a narrative theme suggesting that a psychological flaw undermines the hope for harmony in universal race relations. The play is in certain ways also uniquely self-critical of black racial assumptions without directly rejecting these assumptions.

The Honorable Elijah Muhammad, founder of the Nation of Islam (the 'Black Muslims') of the USA, is usually credited with being the author of this myth which attributes the creation of the white race to the result of a botched experiment by a black scientist in the ancient past. The version of this myth created for the stage by Baraka presents a group of strikingly informal though colourful, comic-strip type characters of an ancient order of black magicians, and depicts the creation of the white race as being the result of a semi-conscious error by a mischievous magician Jacoub, who bears the same name as Elijah Muhammad's black scientist. However, the link between the play and the myth metamorphoses into a more elaborate commentary as Baraka introduces two powerful elements of fictive imagination into the story. The theme of sexual corruption re-surfaces tragically as does the issue of racial harmony and religious responsibility. These themes are hidden within a profusion of linguistic acrobatics, and Baraka's poetic sensibilities come to the fore in the protest speeches given to Nasafi, one of the magicians, who tries to let Jacoub understand and accept the enormous error of his creation of the 'white monster'. In this work Baraka appears to be striving to build a sensationalist structure in order to shock, rather than entertain, the audience.

His directions for the music to be used in the play are specific as he calls for Sun Ra's compositions, and recorded performances, to be played as an integral element of the work. This defines the surreal, and timeless, atmosphere which he intends the events depicted to be enshrouded in. *A Black Mass* represents one of the most adventurous attempts by anyone writing in the USA in that period, or since, to bring the explosive radicalism which was unleashed by the power of black creativity in the civil rights movement into the mainstream of artistic expression in America.

Great Goodness of Life, the third play in this anthology, is in many ways a throw-back to Baraka's work from an earlier period. This work which he dedicates to his 'father with love and respect', and which is subtitled 'A Coon Show' is certainly one of the most impressive and yet painful considerations of the issue of how differing perceptions of class and racial realities across generations have merged into a trauma of spiritual falsity. Characterization is less surreal and impromptu in this work even though the form of the play is extremely imaginative. The interrogator of the main character is never seen. Court Royal, the main character, is the archetypal 'Uncle Tom', a 'decent hard-working post office worker' who suddenly discovers that he is on trial for his life for reasons which he cannot fathom. His personal attitude to life is redolent of procrastination in the black community over the issue of when and where protest is appropriate and what values represent truth in the community. Baraka deals with this painful subject in a manner that suggests that the questions which arise from this emanate from deep wounds within his own psyche.

In his early poetry these concerns were treated as elements of self-examination. In his revolutionary plays Baraka has stretched these concerns to implicate specific elements of the Afro-American community in a wide-ranging indictment of the violation of the unity of spirit of human existence by the divisive imbalance of racial disorder in American society. *Great Goodness of Life* is an extraordinarily belligerent expression of these themes. Tragedy and psychological pain are the fundamental themes examined here on a broad level, but the specific issue of generational distress gives the work a special cachet. Court Royal is a recognizable, though one-dimensional, character, and the voice of his interrogator is an aural symbol of vital power.

This is a play that works as argument as well as presentation. It is a prescient and prophetic work.

The final work in the anthology, *Madheart*, exemplifies the deliberately conscious quest for new forms and primary processes of moral instruction which engaged Baraka at the time when he wrote these works. The theme of sexual despair and emotional distrust between black men and women in American society is treated here as the functional symbol of a specifically tragic history. Baraka's characters are cartoon figures placed in the core of a specific nightmare. He sees the emergence of sexual politics in the black community as a symptom of distress rather than as a sensual outpouring of either love or passion, and this work is an elaborate drama of rejection.

On the page this work is impressive as a literary exercise. On-stage it must develop a life of its own stretching it beyond the limitations of form and attitude imposed by the arbitrary violence of its images and its presumptions. The language borders on the irrational and the improvisatory, utilizing a cascade of imagery from the intellectual baggage of western cultural associations which Baraka presents as the factors which control the sexual and romantic predilections of the 'black man'. Here the characters have no names. They are symbolic predators in a turbulent battle for each other's minds and bodies, and the play presents a picture of a community in turmoil seeking to find peace in harmony between the sexes.

Readers of these works need to be able to hear, and comprehend, the resonances of musical and linguistic adventure which emerged out of the social upheavals in the USA in the sixties, in order to appreciate the vitality which Baraka brought through them to dramatic writing in American theatre. They are principally expressions of

faith in the power of creative truth to expose, and overcome, the falsehoods of personal despair. As such they represent some of Baraka's most impressive achievements in a literary career replete with constant innovation, self-examination, and spiritual regeneration. His transformation from introspective poet to public political activist and social critic injected a sense of the imperative relevance of artistic responsiveness into the pantheon of Afro-American cultural associations on a massive scale.

Baraka's essays on music which have come to be regarded as important signposts for the understanding of the civil rights revolution and the relevance of racial self-assertion to that movement, can now be recognized as the rational element in his work tempering the almost schizophrenic irrationality which he depicted in his plays. As a result of this dichotomy of intellectual prescience emerging from the mind of a single individual, studies of Baraka's work and assessments of his influence on the broader cultural experience in America have often concentrated on the relevance of the viewpoints which he brought to fruition in the period when he wrote these plays and helped to develop the 'black revolutionary theatre'.

It was also this period of his creative growth that gave birth to an impressive, though constantly beleaguered, entry into community activism on his part. He worked to get black officials elected to local offices in Newark, New Jersey, his hometown, and was singularly helpful in getting the first black Mayor elected there as well. His public utterances and actions sometimes seemed to duplicate his stage directions. He was tried and found guilty of incitement on the basis of quotes from some of his plays read out in court by the prosecutor, and then he was acquitted on appeal. This made Baraka a hero of the free speech movement precisely as a consequence of the work which is published here.

Although Baraka continues to write, his theatrical output has become more emphatically didactic and less creative. He has published more essays and biographical work in recent years and he is now a respected elder statesman of the black community in the USA. He teaches various historical and sociological courses, linked with literary and other artistic observations based on his life experiences, in many universities around the USA. In many ways Baraka has become one of his own characters, a symbol of the constant struggle to come to terms with historical realities generated by the multi-racial maelstrom of the urban communities in the USA which provide the psychological setting for these plays.

Lindsay Barrett
Cambridge, UK

INTRODUCTION

a

What can I tell you about the world that you don't already know. Nothing. You know everything. You are everybody. You thought it up before I said it. Sure. You knew it all the time. So why even bother to read the plays. Just go on with the bullshit you call your life. Unless you killing white people, killing the shit they've built, don't read this shit, you won't like it, and it sure won't like you.

b

Trees talk death stones fly meat kills
the key is life in a sun face eye growing devils and angels

the balance is nigger-leroys
the change is the egyptian phenomenon
the change from black to white reversed is the change from
  white to black

the cities of the continent will change hands
the power on the continent will change hands

get in touch with Madbear
'hello, mad bear, what's happening?'

get in touch with Karenga and Tierinja
'Hey now, Hey now, *Habari Gani*'

get in touch with the change, right now, athlete
the statues change from white to black
we are winners and we will win from these devils all this
  land

this is an introduction to a book of plays
i am pophesying the death of white people in this land
i am prophesying the triumph of black life in this land,
and over all the world

we are building publishing houses, and newspapers, and
armies and factories

we will change the world before your eyes,

izm-el-azam,
yes, say it,
say it

sweet nigger
i believe in black allah
governor of creation
Lord of the worlds

As Salaam Alaikum
Amiri Baraka

EXPERIMENTAL DEATH UNIT 1

For a used-to-be dead sister

Experimental Death Unit 1 was first performed at the St Mark's Playhouse, New York City, USA, on March 1, 1965, with the following cast:

DUFF, A WHITE MAN	Dude looked like Steve McQueen
LOCO, A WHITE MAN	Gary Haynes
WOMAN	Barbara Ann Teer
LEADER	James Spruill
FIRST SOLDIER	Walter Jones
SECOND SOLDIER	Gary Bolling

The play was directed by LeRoi Jones.

Scene: Third Avenue. Late winter.

DUFF: (*barely high on heroin, eyes batting*) Well, sufferer, my windows are as icy as the rest of the world.

LOCO: (*whistling softly, and bobbing in his suede shoes*) Is that a form of compromise? From dancing, into the deep sleep of tolerance?

DUFF: A parade of motives. (*Going to look in someone's low window*) Any caution will sense the slant of the world. How to get in on what's, shall we say, out there. (*Laughing slyly*) There are bunches of good things to eat.

LOCO: So our music is time's, and the time of the motive is the time of reallest consciousness. Music. Basketball. Staring in some whore's eyes.

DUFF: I'm sacred as anyone and I say the world is to the man who will take it.

LOCO: And perhaps you are right.

DUFF: You're, unlike the nightingale, a sob sister . . . a helpmate to the weak.

LOCO: You disapprove of life.

DUFF: No. That's not true. You do not know what life . . . if my definition holds, the life of beautiful things . . . you do not know what it is.

LOCO: I despise beauty. What you mean by that. I hate these fools who walk around and call themselves artists, whose sole connection with anything meaningful is the alcohol decay of their skins. Weak dope dripping out of their silky little beards.

DUFF: You have no respect for the world. No understanding of what is of value in it.

LOCO: I respect everything. Existence is self-expression . . . artists are freaks.

DUFF: They are necessary for the world to continue.

LOCO: They are as necessary as anything else, as even freaks are.

DUFF: Don't you respect knowledge?

LOCO: Only when it means intelligence?

DUFF: The open sore! (*He raises an imaginary glass in toast*)

LOCO: The open sore, in the blizzard. (*Raises hand*)

Negro WOMAN *in blue slouch hat steps out of doorway. She is staggering a little, wined up, with one stocking drooping. She could probably have been an attractive woman, in another life. About forty, still gallantly seductive.*

WOMAN: Ho, boys. (*She draws closer*) Hey babarebop . . . two sports.

DUFF: What have we here?

WOMAN: I am a groovy black lady . . . fresh outta idea alley. You dig?

LOCO: I am, shall we say, a digger.

DUFF: But he is a homosexual, so you're wasting your time.

WOMAN: Oh . . . shit . . . one of them. Why you have to be walkin' around my turf?

LOCO: Aw, miss, I ain't no homosexual.

DUFF: I'm just eager.

WOMAN: For what? Your dick up my butt? (*Looks up, smiling*) Drizzle, drizzle, drizzle, drizzle, drizzle. Ah, drizzle. Go head . . . do that right, now! (*At them*) The weather. Your faces. My stories. What are they in terms of spirit? Aside from droopy personalities that will inhabit the street's longing. We whores. We poets. We wet buttocks in the face of God. We all look, and long, and sing.

LOCO: Consider me a ready youth. Made to be used, under and because of you.

DUFF: I differ, unfair lady, only in the sense of my use. I am to be used in all your vacancies. All those holes in your body I want to fill. I got meat and mind to do it with. I mean out there in the street. I'll throw you down . . . mount you, giddyap! giddyap! big-assed nigger lady! . . . then I ride you right out through the rain . . . maybe licking your neck.

WOMAN: You lick your mother's neck! (*Softens*) But lick mine too. In this terrible charlieland.

DUFF: Are you what you look like?

LOCO: (*shivering towards the WOMAN*) Is she what she looks like? Why don't you shrivel in your seltzer-water come, you arrogant know-nothing. She's lovely. Her wet thighs make prints under the skirt.

DUFF: How much are you charging, pilgrim?

WOMAN: I charge just what you owe.

DUFF: Owe?

LOCO: You fool, we owe everything. (*Falls towards WOMAN on his knees, with high whimper, finally tears*)

WOMAN: (*screams*) OWE! OWE! (*She grabs at DUFF's balls*) Everything. What there is to take. (*Laughs*) From what remains of your dwindling stash.

DUFF: You whore. What're you . . . symbolic nigger from the grave?

LOCO: (*turning to restrain* DUFF) Shut up . . . shut up. . . . This is the time your feebleminded muse, and mother . . . dippy wife, brother should have screamed through the snot of their Wheaties.

DUFF: A whore. A black stinking mess of a bitch.

WOMAN: Eat me, you lousy democrat!

LOCO: (*grabbing the* WOMAN*'s legs, as he writhes, though genteely, on the floor*) Help! (*Begins to lick her legs and other flesh*) Help! Help! Help us, nigger. Help us, slick pussy lady. Let me eat your sanity, gobble your gooky mystiques. Lick you. Let me lick you lick you lick you lick you. I'm in an icebox. Heat! Silence! No noise between your hams. Lick and lick. Help, hairy lady. Smelly lady. Blackest of all ladies, help me . . . us! . . . all of us!

DUFF: Get up, you immigrant louse! Spineless! (*Dragging* LOCO *under the armpits away from the* WOMAN) Get away from that greasy . . .

LOCO: I am right, Duff . . . let me go! I know what's needed. I feel it. (*Screams, long long barely human*) Please. I'm right. We die without this heat.

WOMAN: (*regarding both of them haughtily, taking out marijuana, beginning to pull it up into her mouth, sucking deep*) Whhhh . . . shit, damn queers. Whhhh. . . .

(*Sucking, fondling the joint*) Whhhh . . . shit. Fools.

DUFF: Shut up or I'll beat your head into some delicacy!

WOMAN: Dumplings and caviar. Ahhh! Maybe chase it with a little thunderbird! (*A little abstracted*) While I dry out my drawers, and rub out the stains. That would be good.

DUFF: (*advances suddenly, striking the* WOMAN) You whore . . . don't get strange with me.

WOMAN: Ahhh man, the old folks talked about spirits. *The* Spirit! I'll go mystical when I goddam please . . . even while . . . and if . . . you get your big pimple face pushed up hard between my legs. I'll be off somewhere then, thinking about something that would make you mad. What I care about you? Huh . . . your mother and father eat meat with their hands. I saw them old Robin Hood pictures. You can't tell me nothin'.

LOCO: (*recovering slightly*) I will kiss her. I will. I love her. I want to touch her.

DUFF: (*holding him away*) For Christ sakes, you little wop spic kike, get up and stand on your own two feet. (*Half whispering*) I've opened a charge account in your name.

LOCO: (*straightening*) And now you'll swear there's a God?

DUFF: Yes, friend. (*Letting* LOCO *up, and shaking his hand . . .*

brushing off his clothes) You bet there's a God.

WOMAN: Yeh, I agrees to that. There's a God all right . . . but diggit . . . he's a jive ass motherfucka!

Thunder and lightning, the storm increases. Loud and specific thunder.

DUFF: (*screaming in laughter*) You see . . . you see. . . . Thunder thunder big heavy God. My God. God of my fathers.

WOMAN: (*throwing her hands up with her mouth open for rain . . . screaming at thunder*) Yessssssssssssssss. His God. His God. If that's all there is up there, then kill me now. If you can. If that's what you do. (*Pause a moment, now matter-of-factly to DUFF*) Shit, man, must be something else up there. Something else!

LOCO: Madam, madam . . . I love you . . . I want to roll around with you in calm afternoons . . . remember that. But God is (*pointing*) up there! And I believe He knows what's best.

WOMAN: I'm best! Me. My big black thighs. You lay in here and find out how much anybody else got to do with it. I'll fuck your eyeballs out. And your friend's too.

DUFF: The lyric venereal! All hail, the change, and sport of kings. Whoring! And so we'll follow . . . maybe . . . if your price is right . . . that's cheap . . . and your bed is warm . . . and you have some nice things to tell us.

LOCO: Yes, if we do it . . . we have a right to feel right too.

WOMAN: Give me some money . . . and pile on . . . champs.

DUFF: Where's your rooms?

WOMAN: No rooms . . . just that hallway. (*Backs into hallway*) Come on in. (*Starts to undress*) Come on in. Strip down.

DUFF: No rooms? Then we don't buy. We don't need this kind of sordid thing.

LOCO: Please, Duff. I've got something inside me that's got to be put in her. Please. In the hallway.

DUFF: For God's sake . . . don't you value your birthright? In the hallway, Christ . . . think on it closely.

LOCO: Not thought. Just move. Move. (*Grabbing DUFF's face in his hands*).

DUFF: (*pulling away*) Then go, sink into that filthy pussy. You do that. (*Turns to go*).

WOMAN: You come back, hypocrite. You want it as bad as he do.

DUFF stops, turns but does not return. Stands looking.

LOCO: Lady, lady, lady. (*Goes, sinks down on her*) Help me. Help . . . me!

WOMAN: O.K., daddy, O.K., you just do what you can. We'll see . . . We'll.

He pushes his head under her skirts back in the shadows of the hall. DUFF watches for a while squirming, then he begins to take off his pants, and the rest of his clothes. He goes into the hallway and tries to pull the other man off.

DUFF: Get off, you whore face . . . get off . . . the thing's hard . . . I can't wait for your greasy pleasure . . . get off!

WOMAN: (*screech-laughing, shouting*) Yeh . . . it's good booty . . . you better fight over it . . . good good booty. Come on, tall fella . . . you get in here and get your own tongue in. Yeh . . . it's good pussy . . . it's very good pussy. Hahahahahahahahahah!

LOCO: Wait a second, Duff . . . just a second . . . I'm ready to burst . . . just a few seconds more. Please!

DUFF: No, you get up . . . you been there too long . . . I gotta go. . . . Now!

They scuffle, with the screaming. Now there are drums heard in the background, regular, like a military march. Then there are singing voices. Finally, DUFF pulls LOCO out of the hallway and begins to beat him with his heavy boot. He clubs until the boy is bleeding unconscious.

WOMAN: Kill him! Kill him! Yeh. Do it.

Laughs. DUFF finishes, then throws the shoe away and leaps into the hallway on the WOMAN, *who is still screaming 'Kill him! Yeh. Do it!'*

DUFF: Now, I'll deal with you, woman. See how deep I plunge!

WOMAN: Yeh. You kill him . . . now we see . . . we find out. . . . (*Laughs*).

Now a group of long-haired bearded Negro youths marches out with drums and marching cadence, though they look weary and full of combat. At the front of the group one boy marches with a pike on the top of which is a white man's head still dripping blood. They stop in front of the dead boy's body. Then the LEADER *turns as* DUFF *and the* WOMAN *are noticed.*

LEADER: Come out of there!

DUFF: Who's there? What do you want?

LEADER: (*going up to hallway*) Come out, or I'll send someone in to drag you out.

WOMAN: Ahh, honey . . . it's just a soulbrother . . . don't worry. I'll cool everything out. (*Coming out. Louder*) Hey y'all . . . what's happening?

She crawls out of the hallway. DUFF *comes out next, staggering a bit, and bloody.*

DUFF: Who are these?

WOMAN: Hey, cats, what's to it?

LEADER: (*looking the* WOMAN *up and down very slowly. He turns and beckons at the other soldiers*) Who are you?

WOMAN: Nobody, baby . . . nobody at all. . . . Who are you?

DUFF: What do you fellows want? (*Sees head*) God! What's happened?

LEADER: O.K.

WOMAN: O.K., what . . . what's happening, man . . . why you bein' so cool? (*Other soldiers raise guns, begin shooting at the two*) Hey . . . who are you, huh? What you think you in to . . . (*Falls, terribly surprised, ignorant*) Who are you . . . huh . . . why you bein' so cool. . . ?

DUFF: Niggers! Niggers! Niggers! Niggers! Niggers! (*Falls; one of the soldiers comes over and makes sure*)

LOCO: (*stirs. Raises his head, unseeing*) A little pussy. A little heat, that's all. Jus' a little heat! (*LEADER comes over to him. Looks at him a long time*) Just heat. Let me like it in. I need it, baby, I need what you got to give me. Please, please give it to me . . . please. (*He falls, dead*)

LEADER: (*looking, and stooping to make sure the man is dead*) A little pussy. You bet! (*He signals to the army, and they straighten up. He gestures to one soldier, who goes over and cuts the white men's heads off. Another soldier fits them on two poles. The bodies are pushed in a heap. The soldiers are ready*) Ten-hup forwardddd . . . march. . . .

They begin to leave. . . . Last troops leave. Overheard from last ranks:

FIRST SOLDIER: Hey man, that bitch look just like your mother.

SECOND SOLDIER: Man, I'll cut your joint off if you start that stuff. I don't play them kinda games.

FIRST SOLDIER: Yeh, but you'll pat your foot!

When troops leave, bodies are slumped together on stage for some seconds, singing is heard, and the counting of cadence. BLACK.

A BLACK MASS

For the brothers and sisters of The Black Arts

A Black Mass was first performed at Proctor's Theatre, Newark, New Jersey, in May, 1966, with the following cast:

BLACK MAGICIANS:

NASAFI	Yusef Iman
TANZIL	Barry Wynn
JACOUB	Marvin Camillo

WOMEN:

EULALIE	Vionne Doyle
OLABUMI	Olabumi Osafemi
TIILA	Sylvia Jones
THE BEAST	Bob Davis

The play was directed by LeRoi Jones.

Scene: Jet blackness, with maybe a blue or red-violet glow. Soft peaceful music (Sun Ra). Music of eternal concentration and wisdom. Some lights come up, outline the three magicians. Three BLACK MAGICIANS. *They are dressed in long exquisite robes, one with skullcap, one with fez, one with African hat (fila). The outline of some fantastic chemical laboratory is seen, with weird mixtures bubbling, colored solutions (or solutions that glow in the dark).*

NASAFI *hums along with music, voice reaches out occasionally to fill the whole laboratory. Second magician nods his head, beats in tune, absentmindedly, to the music and singing. Third magician intent on what he is doing, with a large book in his hand. He is bent over a mortar and is jamming a pestle into it, watching very closely. The other two also have things they are doing, but in a more leisurely, casual way.*

Signs in Arabic and Swahili on the wall. Strange drawings, diagrams of weird machines. Music can fill the entire room, swelling, making sudden downward swoops, screeching.

NASAFI: These are the beauties of creation. (*Holding large bowl aloft. It glows softly gold in the dim light*) The beauties of strength of our blackness, of our black arts.

TANZIL: Is the mass completed?

NASAFI: Not completed, brother, but the potion is ready. All who taste it will dance mad rhythms of the eternal universe until time is a weak thing.

TANZIL: Until time, that white madness, disappears. Until we have destroyed it and the animals who bring it into the world.

NASAFI: Animals are ourselves. We brought those animals from somewhere. We thought them up. We have deserved whatever world we find ourselves in. If we have mad animals full of time to haunt us, to haunt *us*, who are in possession of all knowledge, then we have done something to make them exist. Is that right, brother Jacoub? (*JACOUB is lost in his meditations*) Is that right, brother Jacoub? (*Notices*) Jacoub. You're off somewhere. Oh, back into that experiment. What is it you're doing?

JACOUB: Oh, the same thing, brother. Creating a new organism. I've been working on this for some time.

TANZIL: We know. We watch you, and wonder. We wonder what you're doing. And what you're thinking. Though we know anyway.

NASAFI: You deal in a strange logic, brother Jacoub. You spoke once of time and we forgot about it. Now there are animals who hiss time madness in the air, and into our lives. I had forgotten (*Turns to TANZIL*) but now I'm sure it was you, Jacoub.

JACOUB: Yes. It was my work. I told you about time. What it

meant. Why I was working in that direction.

TANZIL: Yes, you told us. We respect your knowledge, brother. But time is an animal thing.

JACOUB: Animals do not know time. It is a human thing. A new quality for our minds.

NASAFI: But deadly. It turns us into running animals. Forced across the planet. With demon time in mad pursuit. What good is that? What does it bring to us that we need?

TANZIL: We have no need for time. In fact, brother, we have hatred for it. It is raw and stays raw. It drives brothers across the earth (*Pause*) I think it is evil.

JACOUB: Can knowledge be evil?

NASAFI: Knowledge is knowledge. Evil is evil. But all things in the world are interchangeable. In the endless procession of meaning.

TANZIL: You know this, Jacoub.

JACOUB: (*turns to other magicians*) I know that we are moving at thousands of miles an hour. In endless space. In black endless space. And that this is beautiful reality. But I also know we must find out everything.

NASAFI: We already know everything.

JACOUB: That is not possible.

TANZIL: We know everything, Jacoub.

NASAFI: What we do not know, does not exist. We know without knowing, because there is nothing to know. Everything is everything.

JACOUB: And so I will on where I am moving. Where my eternal mind takes me. Into the voids of black space where new meaning lives.

NASAFI: There is no new meaning. We are your brothers, and we know everything.

TANZIL: It is a fool's game to invent what does not need to be invented.

JACOUB: Let us be fools. For creation is its own end.

NASAFI: (*laughs, low, rising to high hysteria*) We know the myths, Jacoub. We know the realities. We know what is evil and what is perfection. We know we are black and beautiful, speeding through the universe at thousands of miles an hour. We know beyond knowing, knowing there is nothing to know. And knowledge is repetition, and the bringing forth again of things that were so anyway. Everything already exists. You cannot really create.

JACOUB: I am creating. I have created. I made time.

TANZIL: You made animals who vomit time. And we must destroy them. You know that.

JACOUB: I created. I brought something into space that was never there. I will crowd the universe with my creations.

NASAFI: Jacoub, you speak of a magic that is without human sanction. A magic that would rupture the form of beautiful knowledge of beautiful world . . . you speak a madness which I know you create yourself. You want something that will release this madness from within your sainted heart. Why do you punish yourself with such flights? You are black and full of humanity. Yet you move into the emptiness of Godlessness. You are God, yet you destroy your heart with a self that has no compassion, with a self-mind that denies the order and structure of the universe of human signs.

JACOUB: I speak of movement. Of creation. Of making. Of thought.

NASAFI: Then you speak of humanity. Of the human mind.

JACOUB: I speak of things, of knowledge that is beyond the human mind.

TANZIL: If it is beyond the human mind, how will you create it? You are the human mind. No more. Though that is everything.

JACOUB: Those animals of time, though they be evil, are creation. From beyond the human mind.

TANZIL: Not so. You made them. Human. You made them.

And now they roost in the human mind. And by the human mind they will be destroyed.

NASAFI: It is evil to pursue creation even into the lost spaces of the universe. What you bring back will be of no benefit to man. Remember the old myths, brother. The forbidden fruit of madness.

TANZIL: Yes. Though we turn earth into gold and cause the sun's rays to turn our engines. What you call thought is the projection of anti-humanity. The compassionless abstractions, the opposites. The mirror image of creation, turned and distorted, given power, by the forces of good, though these forces breed hell itself.

NASAFI: Jacoub. You are working at what task now?

JACOUB: I told you. Thought. The creation of new energy. Yes. New energy, and new beings.

NASAFI: What?

JACOUB: Yes, brother. I have created time. Now I will create a being in love with time. A being for whom time will be goodness and strength.

TANZIL: This is animal sense. This is a magic against humanity, Jacoub.

NASAFI: Those animals you created are evil. They are the breeders of time. What beasts will you call forth who love such evil?

JACOUB: I will create only one, my brothers.

NASAFI: One what?

JACOUB: A man like ourselves, though different because it will be beyond the human imagination.

TANZIL: And beyond human feeling. A gross distortion of the powers of righteousness.

Bright flames flicker in the background, and go down.

JACOUB: A man like ourselves, yet separate from us. A neutral being.

NASAFI: Neutral being. What madness is this? How can a being be neutral?

JACOUB: Neutral because we, I, have created him, and can fill him as I will. From beyond the powers of natural creation, I make a super-natural being. A being who will not respond to the world of humanity. A being who will make its own will and direction. A being who will question even you and I, my brothers. A being who will be like us, but completely separate. Can you understand?

WOMEN run in screaming. Writhing. Twisting in their thin garments.

WOMEN: Magicians. Magicians. Magicians. Ohhhhhh. Ohhhhhh. Magicians. Black magicians. . . . What fault has our life created?

TIILA: There is evil backing the sky.

EULALIE: The stars are out in daytime.

OLABUMI: The night is filled with thousands of suns.

NASAFI: What? What is this? What are you women doing running into this sanctuary?

EULALIE: The elements disturb us, Lord Magician. The elements threaten us.

OLABUMI: The sky is not the sky. The earth trembles beneath our feet.

TIILA: The sea shudders and rages, and throws strange creatures on the land.

TANZIL: Jacoub. (*Advances towards him*) What is this? (*Consulting his book which he has dangling from his waist*) Do these things have to do with your experiments?

JACOUB: I have no way of knowing. What I do sets off things beyond our reasoning.

NASAFI: Of course it is your experiment. What do you hope to create?

JACOUB is mixing his final solution. Lights go out. Blasts of flame. The WOMEN scream.

WOMEN: Magicians. Why are we so frightened? There is evil riding in the air.

TIILA: Mad visions in the blackness. Oh no. Magicians. Take care.

JACOUB: Now is the time of creation. I enter one solution in the other. (*Screaming*) The blood flows in my head and fingers. The world is expanding. I create the new substance of life. Aiiiieeee.

Bright explosion flashes and a siren-like laughter blasting . . . The laboratory is intense red, then hot violent white. The sirens go up to ear-breaking pitch. The WOMEN *scream.*

NASAFI: Jacoub! Jacoub!

TANZIL: Brother. . . . Brother Jacoub . . . what have you done?

The sirens, screams, and blasting lights are sustained for a few seconds, silhouettes against the white flames that begin to dart around the laboratory. Another intense explosion, the room is silent and dark, and then a sudden hot white glare.

Jacoub?

WOMEN: Oooooh. . . . The earth is alien. Our mothers are sick. The world has shrunk and is choking us.

Explosions.

NASAFI: Deathfire.

JACOUB: No, lifefire. Lifefire. My brothers!

TANZIL: Jacoub, I fear we teeter above the actual horrible void.

Now the glare, glowing wild bright, seems to split. The sound is like glass being scraped on a blackboard. A crouched figure is seen covered in red flowing skins like capes. He shoots up, leaping straight off the stage screaming Sun Ra music of shattering dimension. The figure is absolutely cold white with red lizard-devil mask which covers the whole head and ends up as a lizard spine cape. The figure screams, leaping and slobberlaughing through the audience.

BEAST: I white. White. White. White. (*Leaps, coming to stiffness, then screams stupidly*) White! White! White! (*Hops like beast goon, making horrible farting sounds with his mouth*) White! White! White! (*Hops back towards stage, and up*) White!

As he leaps on stage, he begins to vomit terribly, licking his body where the vomit lands, and vomiting horribly. The WOMEN *begin to scream uncontrollably. The smoke is clearing, and the white thing hops and shudders, vomiting occasionally, and trying to make other explanatory speech-like sounds, but all that comes out intelligibly is the same phrase 'White! White! White!' Then he gurgles off into unintelligible 'explanations'.* JACOUB *is standing stiff, watching his creature. Then he moves forward tentatively, his arms spreading. The creature still leaps and hops, though now less violently, his cries growing to gurgles and slobbers.* JACOUB *is moving forward. The thing is still trying to frighten the audience.*

JACOUB: Brothers. . . . Brothers. . . . Look at this. . . . LOOK AT THIS. . . .

NASAFI and TANZIL are moving away from the creature and JACOUB. Both the magicians are drawing their capes up to their faces. NASAFI rubs his forehead and an eye appears in the middle of his forehead.

NASAFI: It is a monster, Jacoub. That's what you have made. A monster.

JACOUB: It is life, no matter, new life. And strange. Look at it.

TANZIL: (*drawing his elder's whisk, he shakes it, speaking*) *Izm-el-Azam . . . Izm-el-Azam. . . .* (*Repeats over and over*) A mirror of twisted evil. The blind reflection of humanity. This is a soulless beast, Jacoub.

JACOUB: We will teach it.

TANZIL: It will not listen. It has no feeling.

NASAFI: I looked into the wet corridors of the thing's heart, and there was no soulheat. Where the soul's print should be, there is only a cellulose pouch of disgusting habits. (*And with a sudden burst of emotion*) THIS THING WILL KILL, JACOUB. . . . WILL TAKE HUMAN LIFE. . . . (*And the last is long-drawn-out with the terror of the statement*) Jacoub, this creature will take human life . . . because IT HAS NO REGARD FOR HUMAN LIFE!

JACOUB: Brothers, I have created another man.

NASAFI: No, Jacoub. You have created a soulless monster.

The WOMEN scream. Suddenly the BEAST wheels around, facing the terrified black people. Horrible wheezing sounds, still pushed by the same 'White' phrase, gurgle out of his fangs. Tall white bones almost pushing through the 'flesh'. A caveman's loincloth beneath the mask-cape. Sometimes shakes with hideous laughter, staring into its hands, which are webbed, as are its feet. When it is not vomiting it is chewing, and spitting, wheezing and scratching. The BEAST turns, staring at the black people. Wheezing softly, looking into each face. JACOUB has stopped, but spreads his arms in welcome.

JACOUB: (*approaching*) You . . . are. . . .

BEAST: (*in weird parrot-like fashion*) You. . . . You. . . . You. . . . (*Then goes into initial barely intelligible chant*) White! White!

JACOUB: (*pointing to himself*) I. Eye! (*At eye, gesturing*) Me!

BEAST: (*stroking its own chest; slobbering smile crosses its face*) Me! Me! (*A little hop*) Me! . . . White! . . . White! Me! . . . (*A sudden burst of horrible laughter*)

Suddenly the monster turns and begins snarling, then laughing. In high hysterical falsetto. Snarls. Laughs. Then leaps at JACOUB. JACOUB waves his hand and freezes the BEAST behind an invisible wall. Then the BEAST leaps at the WOMEN, grabbing throats or trying to throw open their robes and stick his head in.

TANZIL: (*waves the elder's whisk and a bolt of lightning strikes between the* GIRL *and the* BEAST) *Izm-el-Azam!* Jacoub . . . you have turned loose absolute evil.

JACOUB: How can there be evil in creation, brother? We will teach this thing the world of humanity. And we will benefit by its inhuman. . . .

NASAFI: Benefit? What are you saying? Jacoub . . . you said it . . . this thing is the soulless distortion of humanity.

The BEAST *is standing fixed by black magic, shuddering in terror, but also in a maniacal attempt to free himself from invisible bonds. He grunts his repeated 'White', every now and again punctuating it with a pop-eyed scream, 'Me!' Now one of the young* WOMEN, *attacked by the monster, grabs her throat and begins to stagger.*

TIILA: Magicians. This thing has hurt me. My breath is short. My eyes are turning to stone.

NASAFI: Jacoub.

JACOUB: What is it? What's happening to you?

TANZIL: Oh, Dervish (*head thrown back*), make us strong against this evil!

The WOMAN *stumbles towards* JACOUB, *her face draining of color. Her voice grows coarse, she screams, covering herself with her robes. She emerges, slowly, from within the folds of the garment, her entire body shuddering, and beginning to do the small hop the* BEAST *did. Suddenly she throws back the robes, and she is white, or white blotches streak her face and hair. She laughs and weeps in deadly cross between white and black. Her words have turned to grunts, and she moves like an animal robot.*

TIILA: White! White! (*Her humanity breaks through the dead animal language briefly*) OH LORDS HELP ME I AM TURNED INTO A MONSTER. OH LORDS HEEEEEEEELLLLLLL. . . . (*And then she slumps and begins to hop around, slobbering and scratching*) White! White! White!

The other WOMEN *cringe and moan the* WOMAN*'s name.*

WOMEN: Tiila. . . . Oh Lord, Tiila. . . . What has happened to her? . . . Ohhh . . . evil, evil stalks us.

The BEAST, *seeing the* WOMAN *change from his bite-caress, jiggles and makes obscene movements with his hips, overjoyed. He is still caught in the lightning cage.*

NASAFI: (*sends another thunderbolt, stunning the* WOMAN, *freezing her like the* BEAST. *She moans softly, tearing her body in the trance*) May heaven forgive you, Jacoub! May heaven forgive you!

JACOUB *is trying to minister to the* WOMAN. *But she shrinks away and slobbers unintelligible curses.*

JACOUB: *Izm-el-Azam*! Let the Lord speak to me. Tell me my error. (*In terror at the* WOMAN) This whiteness spreads itself without effort. For the thing is sexless. It cannot breed.

TANZIL: It has merely to touch something to turn it into itself. Or else it sucks out the life juices. Look at our dying sister . . . producing its own hideous image.

JACOUB: Tell me my error.

NASAFI: Jacoub, your error . . . the substitution of thought for feeling. A heart full of numbers and cold formulae. A curiosity for anti-life, for the yawning voids and gaps in humanity we feel sometimes when we grow silent in each other's presence, sensing the infinite millions of miles in the universe, as finite as it is.

TANZIL: Asking God's questions and giving animal answers! We are original reason, and you slip through darkness sliding insanely down those slopes of centuries, endless space, to where the only life is fire burning stone. The cold mineral world. And then, brother, we reach back to warmth and feeling, to the human mind, and compassion. And rise again, back on up the scale, reaching again for the sphere of spheres, back to original reason. To where we always were.

NASAFI: You fell, brother. The monster's eyes are watery, colorless. With endless space beyond. The thing inhabits the voids of reason. Its function was as horrible nothingness. As absence. Of feeling, of thought, of compassion. Out between the stars where life does not exist. This beast is the twisted thing a man would be, *alone* . . . without his human soul.

JACOUB: We will teach it to feel. To love. (*Growing animated*)

TANZIL: It cannot. An animal with its nose quivering.

JACOUB: But it recognized Woman.

TANZIL: Not as the black beautiful lady of our universe, but pure female spoor and meat. An animal with its nose spread open ready to pop the world.

NASAFI: Jacoub, what will you do with this beast? And now the woman . . .

JACOUB: Transport them into the interior laboratory, where I will teach him. The girl . . . there must be some way to restore her life.

TANZIL: This teaching idea is madness, Jacoub. What would you teach an evil spirit?

NASAFI: Yes, perhaps we should cast them out. Perhaps the cold north where we banished the animals of time. In those pits of the earth, the creature might be left to make some horrible life of his own.

WOMEN: Magicians . . . what will you do? Tiila has turned into the beast.

JACOUB: You women should not have invaded this laboratory. You should leave now!

NASAFI: Were any more of you touched by this foulness?

WOMEN: No, Lord. Only Tiila. Only Tiila.

TANZIL: Jacoub. You cannot teach a beast. A blankness in humanity. And we cannot kill. We must set these things loose in the cold north. Where they may find a life in the inhuman cold.

NASAFI: Yes. The beast . . . and sadly, the woman, must be cut off from our people. These things are killers. And smell of the pig.

TANZIL: Sing, women. Sing against this madness and evil. Jacoub. Let the women create their gentle thing here, their rich life smells. Sing, women. Against this sucking death we see. Sing.

The WOMEN, *pulling themselves close to each other, huddled in their fear, raise their voices, at first very softly, with the purring of beautiful pussies. Then they begin to shriek their songs (Sun Ra songs), as if in terror against the two white shivering things quivering in the middle of the laboratory.*

TANZIL: Sing, black women! Sing! Raise your gorgeous souls!

JACOUB: But brothers, we must have compassion, even for evil. We must teach them.

NASAFI: Jacoub. I forbid it. You move against holiness!

JACOUB: No, brother.

TANZIL: Jacoub. You must leave these things in the cold.

JACOUB: But our own Tiila . . .

NASAFI: Look at her. She is not Tiila. She is the void. The evil of blank cold licking the stars.

JACOUB: Even this terror. This inhumanity is conceived, you said, by men. By myself.

NASAFI: There is no self but the breathing world.

JACOUB: And so we shut out part of that world. Part of our lives. Part of knowledge. What is there to desire in the world if we cannot speculate about what we would have exist in it?

TANZIL: There should be no desire but the desire to do away with desire.

NASAFI: This self. This desire. Time. And this white . . . monster.

JACOUB: Man.

NASAFI: Whatever you would call it. Though this thing is not a man. We are men, brother. And this thing is not ourselves. But the hatred of ourselves. Our wholeness. And this self you speak of, and this desire, and the animals of hated time, now these horrible beasts, all these things, Jacoub, set you apart from your brothers. And may God have mercy on your soul.

JACOUB: No, brothers. I will show you. I will begin to teach them. I will have Tiila back. Look. I break the spell and begin to work . . .

NASAFI: No, no, Jacoub . . .

WOMEN: (*their singing turning to screams of horror*) Masters. Magicians. Lord Jacoub. What. . . ?

TANZIL: Jacoub.

JACOUB: (*gesturing*) I will prove the power of knowledge. The wisdom locked beyond the stars. *Izm-el-Azam.*

At JACOUB's gesture, the two beings spring into animation, attacking the magicians and women, killing them with fangs and claws.

JACOUB: (*staggering under the attack, with last breath screams as the beasts close in*) With my last breath I condemn you to the caves. For my dead brothers. May you vanish forever into the evil diseased caves of the cold. . . . Forever, into the caves . . . *Izm* . . . *Izm* . . . *Izm-el-Azam.* May God have mercy. (*Falls*)

The BEASTS howl and hop and then, turning to the audience, their mouths drooling and making obscene gestures, they move out into the audience, kissing and licking peo-

ple as they hop eerily out, still screaming: 'White!. . . . White! Me . . . Me . . . Me . . . White!'

NARRATOR's voice over loudspeaker with low drums and heavy trombones after BEASTS leave.

NARRATOR: And so Brothers and Sisters, these beasts are still loose in the world. Still they spit their hideous cries. There are beasts in our world. Let us find them and slay them. Let us lock them in their caves. Let us declare the Holy War. The Jihad. Or we cannot deserve to live. *Izm-el-Azam. Izm-el-Azam. Izm-el-Azam.* (*Repeated until all lights black*)

GREAT GOODNESS OF LIFE

A Coon Show

For my father with love and respect

Great Goodness Of Life was first performed at Spirit House, Newark, New Jersey, by the Spirit House Movers, in November, 1967. The cast was as follows:

VOICE OF THE JUDGE	David Shakes
COURT ROYAL	Mubarak Mahmoud
ATTORNEY BRECK	Yusef Iman
HOODS 1 &2	Damu
	Larry Miller
YOUNG WOMAN	Elaine Jones
HOODS 3 & 4	Jenga Choma
YOUNG VICTIM	Damu

The play was directed by LeRoi Jones.

Scene: Outside an old log cabin, with morning frost letting up a little.

VOICE: Court.

A man, COURT ROYAL, comes out, grey but still young-looking. He is around fifty. He walks straight, though he is nervous. He comes uncertainly. Pauses.

Come on.

He walks right up to the center of the lights.

Come on.

COURT ROYAL: I don't quite understand.

VOICE: Shut up, nigger.

COURT ROYAL: What? (*Meekly, then trying to get some force up*) Now what's going on? I don't see why I should. . . .

VOICE: I told you to shut up, nigger.

COURT ROYAL: I don't understand. What's going on?

VOICE: Black lunatic. I said shut up. I'm not going to tell you again!

COURT ROYAL: But . . . Yes.

VOICE: You are Court Royal, are you not?

COURT ROYAL: Yes. I am. But I don't understand.

VOICE: You are charged with shielding a wanted criminal. A murderer.

COURT ROYAL: What? Now I know you have the wrong man. I've done no such thing. I work in the Post Office. I'm Court Royal. I've done nothing wrong. I work in the Post Office and have done nothing wrong.

VOICE: Shut up.

COURT ROYAL: But I'm Court Royal. Everybody knows me. I've always done everything. . . .

VOICE: Court Royal you are charged with harboring a murderer. How do you plead?

COURT ROYAL: Plead? There's a mistake being made. I've never done anything.

VOICE: How do you plead?

COURT ROYAL: I'm not a criminal. I've done nothing . . .

VOICE: Then you plead, not guilty?

COURT ROYAL: Of course I'm not guilty. I work in the Post Office. (*Tries to work up a little humor*) You know me, probably. Didn't you ever see me in the Post Office? I'm a supervisor; you know me. I work at the Post Office. I'm no criminal. I've worked at the Post Office for thirty-five years. I'm a supervisor. There must be some mistake. I've worked at the Post Office for thirty-five years.

VOICE: Do you have an attorney?

COURT ROYAL: Attorney? Look, you'd better check you got the right man. You're making a mistake. I'll sue. That's what I'll do.

VOICE: (*laughs long and cruelly*)

COURT ROYAL: I'll call my attorney right now. We'll find out just what's going on here.

VOICE: If you don't have an attorney, the court will assign you one.

COURT ROYAL: Don't bother, I have an attorney. John Breck's my attorney. He'll be down here in a few minutes . . . the minute I call.

VOICE: The court will assign you an attorney.

COURT ROYAL: But I have an attorney. John Breck. See, it's on this card.

VOICE: Will the legal aid man please step forward?

COURT ROYAL: No. I have an attorney. If you'll just call, or adjourn the case until my attorney gets here.

VOICE: We have an attorney for you. Where is the legal aid man?

COURT ROYAL: But I have an attorney. I want my attorney. I don't need any legal aid man. I have money, I have an attorney. I work in the Post Office. I'm a supervisor; here, look at my badge.

A bald-headed smiling house slave in a wrinkled dirty tuxedo crawls across the stage; he has a wire attached to his back, leading offstage. A huge key in the side of his head. We hear the motors 'animating' his body groaning like tremendous weights. He grins, and slobbers, turning his head slowly from side to side. He grins. He makes little quivering sounds.

VOICE: Your attorney.

COURT ROYAL: What kind of foolishness is this? (*He looks at the man*) What's going on? What's your name?

His 'voice' begins some time after the question: the wheels churn out his answer, and the deliberating motors sound throughout the scene.

ATTORNEY BRECK: Pul . . . lead . . . errrr. . . . (*As if the motors are having trouble starting*) Pul . . . pul . . . lead . . . er . . . err . . . guilty! (*Motors get it together and move in proper synchronization*) Pul. . . . Plead guilty, it's your only chance. Just plead guilty, brother. Just plead guilty. It's your only chance. Your only chance.

COURT ROYAL: Guilty? Of what? What are you talking about? What kind of defence attorney are you? I don't even know what I'm being charged with, and you say plead guilty. What's happening here? (*At* VOICE) Can't I even know the charge?

VOICE: We told you the charge. Harboring a murderer.

COURT ROYAL: But that's an obvious mistake.

ATTORNEY BRECK: There's no mistake. Plead guilty. Get off easy. Otherwise thrrrit. (*Makes throat-cutting gesture, then chuckles*) Plead guilty, brother, it's your only chance. (*Laughs*)

VOICE: Plea changed to guilty?

COURT ROYAL: What? No. I'm not pleading guilty. And I want my lawyer.

VOICE: You have your lawyer.

COURT ROYAL: No, my lawyer is John Breck.

ATTORNEY BRECK: Mr Royal, look at me. (*Grabs him by the shoulders*) I am John Breck. (*Laughs*) Your attorney and friend. And I say, plead guilty.

COURT ROYAL: John Bre . . . what? (*He looks at* ATTORNEY *closely*) Breck. Great God, what's happened to you? Why do you look like this?

ATTORNEY BRECK: Why? Haha, I've always looked like this, Mr Royal. Always.

Now another voice, strong, young, begins to shout in the darkness at COURT.

YOUNG VICTIM: Now will you believe me, stupid fool? Will you believe what I tell you or your eyes? Even your eyes. You're here with me, with us, all of us, and you can't understand. Plead guilty you are guilty, stupid nigger. You'll die, they'll kill you and you don't know why, now will you believe me? Believe me, half-white coward. Will you believe reality?

VOICE: Get that criminal out of here. Beat him. Shut him up. Get him.

Now sounds of scuffling come out of darkness. Screams. Of a group of men subduing another man.

YOUNG VICTIM: You bastard. And you Court Royal you let them take me. You liar. You weakling. You woman in the face of degenerates. You let me be taken. How can you walk the earttttt. . . . (*He is apparently taken away*)

COURT ROYAL: Who's that? (*Peers into darkness*) Who's that talking to me?

VOICE: Shut up, Royal. Fix your plea. Let's get on with it.

COURT ROYAL: That voice sounded very familiar. (*Caught in thought momentarily*) I almost thought it was . . .

VOICE: Since you keep your plea of not guilty you won't need a lawyer. We can proceed without your services, counsellor.

ATTORNEY BRECK: As you wish, your honor. Goodbye, Mr Royal. (*He begins to crawl off*) Goodbye, dead sucker! Hahahaha. (*Waving hands as he crawls off and laughing*) Hahahaha, ain't I a bitch . . . I mean ain't I? (*Exits*)

COURT ROYAL: John, John. You're my attorney, you can't leave me here like this. (*Starts after him, shouts*) JOHN!

A siren begins to scream, like in jailbreak pictures. . . . 'Arrrrrrrrrerrrrrr'. The lights beat off, on, in time with the metallic siren shriek. COURT *is stopped in his tracks, bent in anticipation; the siren continues. Machine guns begin to bang bang as if very close to him, cell doors slamming, whistles, yells: 'Break. . . . Break!' The machine guns chatter,* COURT *stands frozen, half-bent arms held away from his body, balancing him in his terror. As the noise, din, continues, his eyes grow until he is almost going to faint.*

COURT ROYAL: Ahhhhhhhgggg. Please. . . . Please . . . don't kill me. Don't shoot me, I didn't do anything. I'm not trying to escape. Please . . . Please PLEEEEEEEAS . . .

The VOICE *begins to shriek almost as loud with laughter as all the other sounds and jumping lights stop as* VOICE *starts to laugh. The* VOICE *just laughs and laughs, laughs until you think it will explode or spit up blood; it laughs long and eerily out of the darkness.*

COURT ROYAL: (*still dazed and staggered, he looks around quickly, trying to get himself together. He speaks now very quietly, and shaken*) Please. Please.

The other VOICE *begins to subside, the laughs coming in sharp cut-off bursts of hysteria.*

VOICE: You donkey. (*Laughs*) You piece of wood. You shiny shuffling piece of black vomit.

The laughter quits like the tide rolling softly back to silence. Now there is no sound, except for COURT ROYAL*'s breathing, and shivering clothes. He whispers. . . .*

COURT ROYAL: Please? (*He is completely shaken and defeated, frightened like a small animal, eyes barely rolling*) Please. I won't escape. (*His words sound corny tinny stupid, dropped in such silence*) Please I won't try again. Just tell me where I am.

The silence again. For a while no movement. COURT *is frozen, stiff, with only eyes sneaking; now they stop, he's frozen, cannot move, staring off into the cold darkness.*

A chain, slightly, more, now heavier, dragged bent, wiggled slowly, light now heavily in the darkness, from another direction. Chains. They're dragged, like things are pulling them across the earth. The chains. And now low chanting voices, moaning, with incredible pain and despair, the voices press just softly behind the chains, for a few seconds, so very very briefly, then gone. And silence.

COURT does not move. His eyes roll a little back and around. He bends his knees, dipping his head, bending. He moans.

COURT ROYAL: Just tell me where I am.

VOICE: HEAVEN.

The VOICE is cool and businesslike. COURT's eyes and head raise an imperceptible trifle. He begins to pull his arms slowly to his sides, and claps them together. The lights dim, and only COURT is seen in dimmer illumination. The VOICE again. . . .

VOICE: HEAVEN. (*Pause*) WELCOME.

COURT ROYAL: (*mumbling*) I never understood . . . these things are so confusing. (*His head jerks like he's suddenly heard Albert Ayler. It raises, his whole body jerks around like a suddenly animate ragdoll. He does a weird dance like a marionette jiggling and waggling*). You'll wonder what the devil-meant. A jiggedy bobbidy fool. You'll wonder what the devil-sent. Diggedy dobbidy cool. Ah man. (*Singing*) Ah man, you'll wonder who the devil-sent. And what was heaven heaven heaven.

This is like a funny joke-dance, with sudden funniness

from COURT; *then suddenly as before he stops frozen again, eyes rolling, no other sound heard . . .*

Now a scream, and white hooded men push a greasy-head nigger LADY *across in front of* COURT. *They are pulling her hair, and feeling her ass. One whispers from time to time in her ear. She screams and bites occasionally, occasionally kicking.*

HOOD 1: (*to the* VOICE) She's drunk. (*Now to* COURT) You want to smell her breath?

COURT ROYAL: (*frightened, also sickened at the sight, embarrassed*) N-no. I don't want to. I smell it from here. She drinks and stinks and brings our whole race down.

HOOD 2: Ain't it the truth!

VOICE: Grind her into poison jelly. Smear it on her daughter's head.

HOOD 1: Right, your honor. You got a break, sister. (*They go off*) Hey, uncle, you sure you don't want to smell her breath?

COURT ROYAL: (*shivers*) No.

VOICE: Royal, you have concealed a murderer, and we have your punishment ready for you. Are you ready?

COURT ROYAL: What? No. I want a trial. Please a trial. I deserve that. I'm a good man.

VOICE: Royal, you're not a man!

COURT ROYAL: Please . . . (*voice breaking*) your honor, a trial. A simple one, very quick, nothing fancy . . . I'm very conservative . . . no frills or loud colors, a simple concrete black toilet paper trial.

VOICE: And funeral.

Now two men in hoods, white work gloves, business suits, very sporty, come in with a stretcher. A black man is dead on it. There is long very piped applause. 'Yea. Yea'.

HOOD 1: It's the Prince, your honor. We banged him down.

VOICE: He's dead?

HOOD 2: Yes. A nigger did it for us.

VOICE: Conceal the body in a stone. And sink the stone deep under the ocean. Call the newspapers and give the official history. Make sure his voice is in that stone too, or . . . (*Heavy nervous pause*) Just go ahead.

HOOD 1: Of course, your honor. (*Looks to* COURT, *almost as an afterthought*) You want to smell his breath?

They go out.

COURT ROYAL: (*mumbling, still very frightened*) No . . . no . . . I have nothing to do with any of this. I'm a good man. I have a car. A home. (*Running down*) A club.

(*Looks up, pleading*) Please there's some mistake. Isn't there? I've done nothing wrong. I have a family. I work in the Post Office, I'm a supervisor. I've worked for thirty-five years. I've done nothing wrong.

VOICE: Shut up, whimpering pig. Shut up and get ready for sentencing. It'll be hard on you, you can bet that.

COURT ROYAL: (*a little life; he sees he's faced with danger*) But tell me what I've done. I can remember no criminal, no murderer I've housed. I work eight hours, then home, and television, dinner, then bowling. I've harbored no murderers. I don't know any. I'm a good man.

VOICE: Shut up, liar. Do you know this man?

An image is flashed on the screen behind him. It is a rapidly shifting series of faces. Malcolm. Patrice. Rev King. Garvey. Dead nigger kids killed by the police. Medgar Evers.

COURT ROYAL: What?

VOICE: I asked you, do you know this man? I'm asking again, for the last time. There's no need to lie.

COURT ROYAL: But this is many men, many faces. They shift so fast I cannot tell who they are . . . or what is meant. It's so confusing.

VOICE: Don't lie, Royal. We know all about you. You are guilty. Look at that face. You know this man.

COURT ROYAL: I do? (*In rising terror*) No. No. I don't. I never saw that man, it's so many faces, I've never seen those faces . . . never . . .

VOICE: Look closer, Royal. You cannot get away with what you've done. Look more closely. You recognize that face . . . don't you? The face of the murderer you've sheltered all these years. Look, you liar, look at that face.

COURT ROYAL: No, no, no . . . I don't know them. I can't be forced into admitting something I never did. Uhhh . . . I have worked. My God, I've worked. I've meant to do the right thing. I've tried to be a . . .

The faces shift, a long slow wail, like a moan, like secret screaming, has underscored the flashing faces. Now it rises sharply to screaming point thrusts. COURT *wheels around to face the image on the screen, directly. He begins shouting loud as the voices.*

COURT ROYAL: No, I've tried . . . please I never wanted anything but peace . . . please, I tried to be a man. I did. I lost my . . . heart . . . please it was so deep, I wanted to do the right thing, just to do the right thing. I wanted . . . everything to be . . . all right. Oh, please . . . please.

VOICE: Now tell me, whether you know that murderer's face or not. Tell me before you die!

COURT ROYAL: No, no. I don't know him. I don't. I want to do the right thing. I don't know them. (*Raises his hands in his agony*) Oh, son . . . son . . . dear God, my flesh, forgive me . . . (*Begins to weep and shake*) My sons. (*He clutches his body, shaken throughout by his ugly sobs*) Dear God . . .

VOICE: Just as we thought. You are the one. And you must be sentenced.

COURT ROYAL: I must be sentenced. I am the one. (*Almost trance-like*) I must be sentenced. With the murderer. I am the one.

VOICE: The murderer is dead. You must be sentenced alone.

COURT ROYAL: (*as first realization*) The murderer . . . is . . . dead?

VOICE: And you must be sentenced. Now. Alone.

COURT ROYAL: (*voice rising, in panic, but catching it up short*) The murderer . . . is dead.

VOICE: Yes. And your sentence is . . .

COURT ROYAL: I must be sentenced . . . alone. Where is the murderer? Where is his corpse?

VOICE: You will see it presently.

COURT ROYAL: (*head bowed*) God. And I am now to die like

the murderer died?

VOICE: No. (*Long pause*) We have decided to spare you. We admire your spirit. It is a compliment to know you can see the clearness of your fate, and the rightness of it. That you love the beauty of the way of life you've chosen here in the anonymous world. No one beautiful is guilty. So how can you be? All the guilty have been punished. Or are being punished. You are absolved of your crime, at this moment, because of your infinite understanding of the compassionate God Of The Cross. Whose head was cut off for you, to absolve you of your weakness. The murderer is dead. The murderer is dead.

Applause from the darkness.

COURT ROYAL: And I am not guilty now?

VOICE: No, you are free. Forever. It is asked only that you give the final instruction.

COURT ROYAL: Final instruction . . . I don't understand . . .

VOICE: Heroes! Bring the last issue in.

The last two hooded men, HOODS 3 and 4, return with a young black man of about twenty. The boy does not look up. He walks stiff-legged to the center in front of COURT. He wears a large ankh around his neck. His head comes up slowly. He looks into COURT's face.

YOUNG VICTIM: Peace.

COURT looks at his face, begins to draw back. The hooded man comes and places his arms around COURT's shoulders.

VOICE: Give him the instruction instrument.

HOOD 3 takes a pistol out of his pocket and gives it with great show to COURT.

HOOD 3: The silver bullet is in the chamber. The gun is made of diamonds and gold.

HOOD 4: You get to keep it after the ceremony.

VOICE: And now, with the rite of instruction, the last bit of guilt falls from you as if it was never there, Court Royal. Now, at last, you can go free. Perform the rite, Court Royal, the final instruction.

COURT ROYAL: What? No. I don't understand.

VOICE: The final instruction is the death of the murderer. The murderer is dead and must die, with each gift of our God. This gift, is the cleansing of guilt, and the bestowal of freedom.

COURT ROYAL: But you told me the murderer was dead already.

VOICE: It *is* already. The murderer has been sentenced. You have only to carry out the rite.

COURT ROYAL: But you told me the murderer was dead. (*Starts to back away*) You told me . . . you said I would be sentenced alone.

VOICE: The murderer *is dead.* This is his shadow. This is his shadow. This one is not real. This is the myth of the murderer. His last fleeting astral projection. It is the murderer's myth that we ask you to instruct. To bind it forever . . . with death.

COURT ROYAL: I don't . . . Why do . . . you said I was not guilty. That my guilt had fallen away.

VOICE: The rite must be finished. This ghost must be lost in cold space. Court Royal, this is your destiny. This act was done by you a million years ago. This is only the memory of it. This is only a rite. You cannot kill a shadow, a fleeting bit of light and memory. This is only a rite, to show that you would be guilty but for the cleansing rite. The shadow is killed in place of the killer. The shadow for reality. So reality can exist beautiful like it is. This is your destiny, and your already lived-out life. Instruct, Court Royal, as the centuries pass, and bring you back to your natural reality. Without guilt. Without shame. Pure and blameless, your soul washed (*pause*) white as snow.

COURT ROYAL: (*falling to his knees, arms extended as in loving prayer, to a bright light falling on him, racing around the space*) Oh, yes . . . I hear you. And I have waited for this promise to be fulfilled.

VOICE: This is the fulfilment. You must, at this moment, enter into the covenant of guiltless silence. Perform the rite, Court Royal.

COURT ROYAL: Oh, yes, yes . . . I want so much to be happy . . . and relaxed.

VOICE: Then carry out your destiny . . .

COURT ROYAL: Yes, yes . . . I will . . . I will be happy. . . (*He rises, pointing the gun straight up at the young man's face*) I must be . . . fulfilled . . . I will.

He fires the weapon into the boy's face. One short sound comes from the boy's mouth.

YOUNG VICTIM: Papa. (*He falls*)

COURT stands looking at the dead boy with the gun still up. He is motionless.

VOICE: Case dismissed, Court Royal . . . you are free.

COURT ROYAL: (*now suddenly to life, the lights go up full, he has the gun in his hand. He drops, flings it away from him*) My soul is as white as snow. (*He wanders up to the body*) My soul is as white as snow. (*He starts to wander off the stage*) White as snow. I'm free. I'm free. My life is a beautiful thing.

He moves slowly toward the edge of the stage, then suddenly a brighter mood strikes him.

COURT ROYAL: (*raising his hands as if calling someone*) Hey, Louise, have you seen my bowling bag? I'm going down to the alley for a minute.

He is frozen, the lights dim to BLACK.

MADHEART

A Morality Play

For the brothers and sisters of
the Black Arts Alliance, San Francisco

Madheart was first performed at San Francisco State College in May, 1967, with the following cast from the Black Arts Alliance:

BLACK MAN	Jimmy Garrett
BLACK WOMAN	Velma Mitchell
MOTHER	Yolande Redfurd
SISTER DEVIL LADY	Elendar Barnes

The play was directed by LeRoi Jones.

DEVIL LADY: You need pain. (*Coming out of shadows with neon torch, honky-tonk calliope music*) You need pain, ol' nigger devil, pure pain, to clarify your desire.

BLACK MAN: (*turns slowly to look at her, raises his arms, straight out, parallel to the floor, then swiftly above his head, then wide open in the traditional gesture of peace*) God is not the devil. Rain is not fire nor snow, nor old women dying in hallways.

DEVIL LADY: There is peace.

BLACK MAN: There is no peace.

DEVIL LADY: There is beauty.

BLACK MAN: None that you would know about.

DEVIL LADY: There is horror.

BLACK MAN: There is horror. There is (*pause, as if to cry or precipitate a rush of words which do not come*) . . . only horror. Only stupidity. (*Raising to point at her*) Your stale pussy weeps paper roses.

DEVIL LADY: And horror.

BLACK MAN: Why aren't you dead? Why aren't you a deader thing than nothing is?

DEVIL LADY: I am dead and can never die.

BLACK MAN: You will die only when I kill you. I raise my hand to strike. (*Pulling out sword*) I raise my hand to strike. Strike. Strike. (*Waving the sword, and leaping great leap*) Bitch devil in the whistling bowels of the wind. Blind snow creature.

A fanfare of drums. Loud dissonant horns. The action freezes. The lights dim slowly, on the frozen scene. The actors fixed. The music rises. Lights completely off. Then flash. On. On. Off. Off. As if it was an SOS signal. Then the music changes, to a slow, insinuating, nasty blues. Rock. Rock. Voices offstage begin to pick up the beat, and raise it to falsetto howl. Scream, in the sensual moan.

VOICES: Rock. Rock. Love. Me. Love. Me. Rock. Heaven. Heaven. Ecstasy. Ecstasy. Oooooahhhhhhummmmmmmmmmah-ah-ahooooooh. Let love. Let rock. Let Heaven. All love. All love, like rock . . .

Lights go full up. Silence. The action continues. The actors from the freeze go to life, but never complete the initial action. As if in slow motion.

BLACK MAN: Hear that? Hear those wild cries? Souls on fire. Fire. Floods of flame. Hear that. Ol' humanless bitch. Dead judge.

DEVIL LADY: I am the judge. I am the judge. (*She squats like an old Chinese*) The judge. (*Rolls on her back, with skirt raised, to show a cardboard image of Christ pasted over her pussy space. A cross in the background*) My pussy rules the world through newspapers. My pussy radiates the great heat. (*She rolls back and forth on the floor, panting*)

BLACK MAN: The great silence. Serenades of brutal snow. You got a cave, lady?

VOICES: Blood. Snow. Dark cold cave. Illusion. Promises. Hatred and Death. Snow. Death. Cold. Waves. Night. Dead white. Sunless. Moonless. Forever. Always. Iceberg Christians, pee in the ocean. Help us. We move.

Music again, over all, the high beautiful falsetto of a fag. The traditional love song completely taking over. Blackout.

Lights up, the DEVIL LADY *lies in the middle of the stage with a spear, or many arrows, stuck in her stomach and hole. As the lights come up, the singing subsides to low hum. Three black women enter slowly (*MOTHER, SISTER, WOMAN*), humming now softly. The* BLACK MAN *is standing just a few feet away from the skewered* DEVIL LADY. *He is gesturing with his hands, at the prone figure, with his hands like he is conjuring or hypnotizing.*

BLACK MAN: You will always and forever be dead, and be dead, and always you will be the spirit of deadness, or the cold stones of its promise. (*He takes up a huge wooden stake and drives it suddenly into her heart, with a loud thud as it penetrates the body, and crashes deep in the floor*) Beautiful. (*Preoccupied, and still unaware of the black women*) Beautiful. (*He makes as if to repeat his act, and one of the women speaks*)

MOTHER: No. Madman. Stop!

SISTER: She is old and knows. Her wisdom inherits the earth. (*Stepping forward suddenly at* DEVIL LADY) I love you. I love the woman in my sleep. I cannot love death.

BLACK WOMAN: Perhaps we are intruding. (*The two other women turn and stare at her, and form a quick back-off circle to point at her casually and turn their heads. The* BLACK WOMAN*'s head is wrapped in a modest gele, and her natural hair cushions her face in a soft remark*) You want the whole thing.

MOTHER: You want the whole thing, baby. (*Advancing*) The earth, the sky.

SISTER: You must leave what the womb leaves. The possibility of all creation.

BLACK MAN: The dead do not sing. Except through the sawdust lips of science-fiction jigaboos, who were born, and disappeared, in a puff of silence at the foot of the Woolworth heir's cement condom.

DEVIL LADY: (*from the floor, moaning through her teeth, from beyond the grave. Let there be music, and setting, to indicate that these words come from behind the veil*) OOOOOOOOOOHHHHHHHHHHH. . . . My pussy throbs above the oceans, forcing weather into the world.

BLACK MAN: The cold.

MOTHER: The light and promise. (*From an ecstatic pose suddenly turns into a barker, selling young black ass*) Uhyehhh. Eh? Step right up. Get your free ass. (*Starts moving, wiggle — suggestively*) Come on, fellahs . . .

SISTER: And free enterprise.

DEVIL LADY: Enter the prize. And I am the prize. And I am dead. And all my life is me. Flowing from my vast whole, entire civilizations.

BLACK WOMAN: (*almost inadvertently*) That smell. I knew I'd caught it before.

BLACK MAN: Broomsticks thrust up there return embossed with zombie gold.

MOTHER: Out of the bowels of the sun. I slap around drunk up Lenox. Stumble down 125th into the poet who frowns at me, lost in my ways. You'd think that ol' nigger was worth something.

SISTER: (*dazed*) It's just . . . just . . . (*Staggers toward the dead woman*) . . . that I wanted to be something like her, that's all. (*Weeps but tries to hold it*)

BLACK WOMAN: Yet she be a stone beast, ladies! A stone ugly pagan. Israelites measure your beauty by what the filthy bitch looks like lying around like an old sore.

BLACK MAN: An old punctured sore with the pus rolled out.

SISTER: (*falling to her knees. Screams*) Aiiiieeeeee . . . it could be me, and backward out of the newspaper dreams of my American life. Out of the television enemas poured through my eyes out of my mouth onto the floor of everybody's life. I hate so. I am in love with my hatred. Yet I worship this beast on the floor, because . . .

BLACK WOMAN: Because you have been taught to love her by background music of sentimental movies. A woman's mind must be stronger than that.

BLACK MAN: A black woman. (*Throws his hands above his head*) A black woman! Wouldn't that be something?

The dead white DEVIL LADY*'s body wiggles in a shudder and releases, dead.*

BLACK WOMAN: (*her voice goes up to high long sustained note*) I am black black and am the most beautiful thing on the planet. Touch me if you dare. I am your soul.

MOTHER: What is wrong with the niggers, this time? I'm old and I hump along under my wig. I'm dying of oldness. I'm dying of the weight. The air is so heavy. (*Taken by more sombre mood*) And dying all the time. Diseased. Broken. Sucking air from dirty places. Your mother. Shit filthiness. In a cheap mink. In a frozen roach funeral.

SISTER: Brazen bitch. You trying to steal my shit?

MOTHER: Make for the exit, child, before you bleed on somebody.

They begin to fight each other. Breathing hard and cursing. The BLACK WOMAN *backs away, hands at her mouth, terrified.*

BLACK WOMAN *comes close to the* BLACK MAN, *as the two women begin to fight in aggravated pantomimed silence. Clock gongs away, maybe fifty times. Slow sudden insinuating drums, and brushes. The two women fighting clutch each other and fight more stiffly, finally subsiding into a frozen posture.*

BLACK WOMAN: What do you want, black man? What can I give you? (*In a calm loving voice*) Is there a heart bigger than mine? Is there any flesh sweeter, any lips fatter and redder, any thighs more full of orgasms?

BLACK MAN: (*leaning towards her*) Sweet pleasure. (*He touches her arm*)

DEVIL LADY: (*beginning to moan on the floor*) Ooooooaaaaa. My white pussy is beating the air. My navel is raw and ready to be attached. I come back from the dead 'cause I wanna.

BLACK MAN: Oh, bullshit. Go back, for chrissakes.

BLACK WOMAN: Christ was a pagan. A stumblebum in the Swedish baths of philosophy.

MOTHER and SISTER struggle suddenly on the floor. With violence and slobbering.

MOTHER AND SISTER: Fuckingbitch Fuckingbitch Fuckingbitch Fuckingbitch Fuckingbitch Fuckingbitch Fuckingbitch Fuckingbitch Fuckingbitch Fuckingbitch Fuckingbitch Fuckingbitch . . .

BLACK WOMAN: Thing on the floor, be still. I'm tired of your ignorant shamble. Let me be alone in the world with women and men, and your kind be still in the grave where you have fun.

DEVIL LADY screams with throbbing thighs. MOTHER and SISTER begin crawling across the floor to the DEVIL LADY. She writhes and stiffens in death. The MOTHER whimpers, the SISTER gags and weeps and whines.

SISTER: My dead sister reflection. Television music. Soft lights and soft living among the buildings.

BLACK WOMAN: She went for luxury.

BLACK MAN: I used to see her in white discotheque boots and sailor pants. (*Pointing to the crawling women*) This is the nightmare in all of our hearts. Our mothers and sisters grovelling to white women, wanting to be white women, dead and hardly breathing on the floor. Look at our women dirtying themselves. (*Runs and grabs wig off* SISTER*'s head*) Take off filth. (*He throws it onto the dead woman's body*) Take your animal fur, heathen. (*Laughs*) Heathen. Heathen. I've made a new meaning. Let the audience think about themselves, and about their lives when they leave this happening. This black world of purest possibility. (*Laughs*) All our lives we want to be alive. We scream for life.

BLACK WOMAN: Be alive, black man. Be alive, for me. For me, black man. (*Kisses him*) And love me. Love. Me.

BLACK MAN: Women, assemble around me. I'm gonna sing for you now, in my cool inimitable style. About my life. About my road, and where it's taking me now. Assemble, sweet black ladies, ignorant or true, and let me run down the game of life.

BLACK WOMAN: Get up, you other women, and listen to your man. This no fattening insurance nigger greying around the temples. This is the soulforce of our day-to-day happening universe. A man.

SISTER: A man. Dammit. Dance. (*Change*) Men. What do they do? Hang out. Niggermen. If I have to have a niggerman, give me a faggot anyday.

MOTHER: (*laughing high voice and sweeping her hand*) Oh, chil', I know the kind you mean. Uhh, so sweet. I tell you. But . . . a white boy's better, daughter. Don't you forget it. Just as sof' and sweet as a pimple. (*Spies* BLACK WOMAN *still standing separate and looking confused, hands covering her ears*) Haha. . . . (*Hunching or trying to hunch* SISTER) Haaha, will you look at that simple bitch. My lan', chil', why don't you straighten up and get in the world?

SISTER: Yeh, Desideria, why don't you make up your mind?

BLACK MAN: What is this? (*To* BLACK WOMAN) What's all this mouth-mouth action? Why don't these women act like women should? Why don't they act like Black Women? All this silly rapping and screaming on the floor. I should turn them over to the Black Arts and get their heads relined.

BLACK WOMAN: They've been tricked and gestured over. They hypnotized, that's all. White Magic.

BLACK MAN: White Magic. Yes. (*Raising his stake suddenly*) Maybe this dead thing's fumes are sickening the air. I'll make sure it's dead. (*He strikes*)

SISTER screams as BLACK MAN stabs the DEVIL LADY.

SISTER: (*grabs her heart as if the man had struck her*) Oh God, you've killed me, nigger.

BLACK MAN: What? (*Wheels to look at her*)

BLACK WOMAN: You're killed if you are made in the dead thing's image, if the dead thing on the floor has your flesh and your soul. If you are a cancerous growth. Sad thing.

SISTER: I'm killed and in horrible agony, and my own brother did it. (*Staggering around stage. Finally falls in great over-dramatic climax*) My own bro . . . ther. (*Falls*)

BLACK MAN: Oh, God! (*Rushes over to her*) Is this child my sister?

BLACK WOMAN: No, get away from her. She is befouled.

BLACK MAN: But my own sister . . . I've killed her.

BLACK WOMAN: She's not even dead. She just thinks she has to die because that white woman died. She's sick.

BLACK MAN: (*stands over SISTER, pondering what the BLACK WOMAN has said*) Hmmmmmm.

MOTHER: You've killed her. You've killed my baby. (*Rushes over to BLACK MAN and starts beating him in the chest. She's weeping loud and disconsolately*) You've killed my own sweet innocent girl. My own sweet innocent girl . . . she never had a chance. She coulda been somebody.

BLACK WOMAN: Woman, you're crazy.

BLACK MAN: I killed my sister. (*Mumbling*)

MOTHER: No, I'm not the crazy one. You all are crazy. Stuntin' like this. All that make-believe. And you killed your own flesh. And this ol' nappy-head bitch agitated the whole shit. (*Weeps*) My baby, she never had a chance. She never even got a chance to be nobody. Oh, God, why's my life so fucked up? And you, man, you killed your own sister. I hope that shit you talk's enough to satisfy you. Or that nappy-head bitch.

BLACK WOMAN: Why don't you find out something before you show how long ignorance can claim a body? An old woman like you should be wise . . . but you not wise worth a mustard seed.

MOTHER: You talk to me with respect, whore . . . or I'll . . . (*Threatening gesture*)

BLACK WOMAN: What? Or you'll beat me with your wig? You're streaked like the devil. And that pitiful daughter of yours is not even dead. But she'll act dead as long as she licks on that devil woman.

BLACK MAN: My mother, my sister, both . . . like television dollbabies, doing they ugly thing. To mean then, me, and what they have for me, what I be then, in spite of my singing, and song, to stand there, or lay there, like they be, with the horizon blowing both ways, to change, God damn . . . and be a weight around my neck . . . a weight . . .

MOTHER: Well, leave us alone, murderer . . . punk ass murderer. Gimme a drink an' shut up. And drag that whore's mouth shut too.

BLACK WOMAN: You shut up. And get back in your dead corner with the other rotting meat.

BLACK MAN: I've killed my sister. And now watch my mother defiled, thrown in a corner.

BLACK WOMAN: If she was your mother, she'd be black like you. She'd come at you to talk to you, about the old south, and ladies under trees, and the soft wet kiss of her own love, how it made you fight through sperm to arrive on this planet whole . . . (*soft laugh*) . . . and beautiful.

BLACK MAN: Who're you . . . to talk so much . . . and to stand apart from this other jive? The lousy score's two to one, diddy-bops!

MOTHER starts singing a sad dirge for the daughter, trailing around the body, throwing kisses at the still figures.

MOTHER: Yohoooooo yohoooooo, daw daw daw daw daw daw daw hodaw hoooodaw deee. All the beauty we missed. All the cool shit. All the sad drinking in crummy bars we missed. All the crossmating and crossbreeding and holy jive in the cellars and closets. The cool flirts in the ladies' meeting. The meeting of the ex-wives. All the Belafontes and Poitiers and hid unfamous nigger formers, hip still on their lawns, and corn and wine, and tippy drinks with green stuff with cherries and white cats with titles, all the television stuff, and tapdances, and the soft music, and stuff. All of it gone. Dead child, save me, or take me. . . . (*She bows, kisses the two bodies*) Or save me, take me with you. . . . Daw daw doooodaw daw ding ding daw do do dooon. . . . (*She trails sadly around the bodies*)

BLACK MAN: This is horrible. Look at this.

BLACK WOMAN: It's what the devil's made. You know that. Why don't you stop pretending the world's a dream or puzzle? I'm real and whole . . . (*Holds out her arms*) And yours, only, yours, but only as a man will you know that.

BLACK MAN: You are . . .

BLACK WOMAN: I'm the black woman. The one who disappeared. The sleepwalker. The one who runs through your dreams with your life and your seed. I am the black woman. The one you need. You know this. Now you must discover a way to get me back, Black Man. You and you alone, must get me. Or you'll never . . . lord . . . be a man. My man. Never know your own life needs. You'll walk around white ladies breathing their stink, and lose your seed, your future to them.

BLACK MAN: I'll get you back. If I need to.

BLACK WOMAN: (*laughs*) You need to, baby . . . just look around you. You better get me back, if you know what's good for you . . . you better.

BLACK MAN: (*looking around at her squarely, he advances*) I better? . . . (*A soft laugh*) Yes. Now is where we always are . . . that now. . . . (*He wheels and suddenly slaps her crosswise, back and forth across the face*)

BLACK WOMAN: What. . . . What . . . oh love . . . please . . . don't hit me. (*He hits her, slaps her again*)

BLACK MAN: I want you, woman, as a woman. Go down. (*He slaps again*) Go down, submit, submit . . . to love . . . and to man, now, forever.

BLACK WOMAN: (*weeping, turning her head from side to side*) Please don't hit me . . . please . . . (*She bends*) The years are so long, without you, man, I've waited . . . waited for you . . .

BLACK MAN: And I've waited.

BLACK WOMAN: I've seen you humbled, black man, seen you crawl for dogs and devils.

BLACK MAN: And I've seen you raped by savages and beasts, and bear bleach shit children of apes.

BLACK WOMAN: You permitted it . . . you could . . . do nothing.

BLACK MAN: But now I can. (*He slaps her, drags her to him, kissing her deeply on the lips*) That shit is ended, woman, you with me, and the world is mine.

BLACK WOMAN: I . . . oh love, please stay with me . . .

BLACK MAN: Submit, for love.

BLACK WOMAN: I . . . I submit. (*She goes down, weeping*) I submit . . . for love . . . please love.

The MAN *sinks to his knees and embraces her, draws her with him up again. They both begin to cry and then laugh, laugh wildly at everything and themselves.*

BLACK MAN: You are my woman, now, forever. Black woman.

BLACK WOMAN: I am your woman, and you are the strongest of God. Fill me with your seed.

They embrace . . . MOTHER *is now crawling around on her knees.*

MOTHER: Tony Bennett, help us please. Beethoven, Peter Gunn . . . deliver us in our sterling silver head-dress . . . oh please deliver us.

BLACK MAN: This is enough of this stuff. Get up, supposed-to-be mother, and drag that supposed-to-be sister up too. This stuff is over and done. Get up or so help me, you die with the dead bitch you worship.

MOTHER: What I care? Batman won't love me without my yellow-head daughter. I'm too old for him or Robin. I can't paint soupcans, the junk I find is just junk, my babies stick in they eyes, I'm sick in the big world, and white shit zooms without me. I'm a good fuck and an intelligent woman . . . frankly . . . frankly . . . (*Laughs. Turns to look at the* BLACK MAN)

Fuck both of you stupid ass niggers . . . you'll never get no light. . . . Daughter . . . Daughter . . . put on your wig and wake up dancing. The old Italian wants you to marry him.

BLACK MAN: Why won't these women listen? Why do they want to die?

BLACK WOMAN: The white one's fumes strangle their senses. The thing's not dead.

BLACK MAN: I've killed it. And death must come to the thing. I'll do it again. (*Shouts*) Die, you bitch, and drag your mozarts into your nasty hole. Your mozarts stravinskys stupid white sculpture corny paintings deathfiddles, all your drawling jive, drag it in and down with you, your office-buildings blow up in your pussy, newspapers poison gases congolene brain stragglers devising ways to deal death to their people, your smiles, your logic, your brain, your intellectual death, go to a dead planet in some metal bullshit, dissolve, disappear, leave your address in the volcano, and turn into the horrible insects of a new planet . . . but leave. I am the new man of the earth, I command you . . . Command bullshit. (*He runs over and stomps the dead* DEVIL LADY *in her face*) This kinda command. (*He drags her over to the edge of the stage, and drops her off*) Into the pit of deadchange, slide bitch slide.

Smoke and light shoot up where she lands.

BLACK WOMAN: Yes yes. . . .

MOTHER: You fool. You crazy thing . . . get out of here.

BLACK WOMAN: Why don't you listen . . . or die, old hag!

BLACK MAN: (*grabs MOTHER by the arm, drags her over to the edge*) Look down in there, smell those fumes. That's ashy death, bitchmother, stinking filthy death. That's what you'll be. Smell it. Look at it!

MOTHER: You fool, you mess with the gods, and shit will belt you.

BLACK WOMAN: Listen, old woman, this is a man speaking, a black man.

MAN shakes the MOTHER violently.

BLACK MAN: Yes, you listen.

MOTHER: No, no . . . (*She pulls away, goes to SISTER, who's now starting to turn over, fan and shake herself*) Get away . . . you've killed my daughter . . . you . . . what, she's still breathing?

BLACK WOMAN: I told you she was . . . 'sick actress from Broome Street'.

MOTHER: Oh, daughter . . . the Italian called you just a while ago. Get up, pussycat, Mama's worried so about you. You hungry? (*She pulls out a box lunch from her brassiere*) You must be starved.

SISTER: (*wakes up, looks around, senses the DEVIL LADY is miss-*

ing, dead) Where . . . where's she . . . ooh . . . Where's my body . . . my beautiful self? Where? What'd you do, you black niggers? What'd you do to me? Where'd you hid me? Where's my body? My beautiful perfumed hole?

MOTHER: The hairy nigger killed you, daughter, dropped you in a . . . pit.

SISTER: What! ooooooooo. . . . (*Horrible shriek*) ooooooo . . . here . . . ooooooo . . . (*Runs towards* BLACK MAN) You beast bastard . . . oooooo . . . Where'd you stick my body. . . ?

BLACK MAN grabs her and tosses her to the floor. MOTHER goes over to comfort her.

MOTHER: Oh, please, pussycat . . . ain't you hungry a little bit? I saved some dinner for you. Eat something, pussycat, baby, don't aggravate yourself. You'll ruin your complexion. Don't let these niggers upset you.

SISTER: Oh, God, I know . . . he's killed me. He's dropped me in that pit. (*Weeps inconsolably*)

BLACK WOMAN: Bitchfool.

SISTER: You jealous 'cause you ain't blond like me, nigger. You shut up and get outta here with that nigger. . . . You get outta here . . . get outta here. So help me I'll kill you . . . get outta here, get outta here, get outta here . . .

Screams, turns into mad raving creature, runs, puts wig back on head, pulls it down over her eyes, runs around stage screaming, MOTHER *chasing her, trying to feed her from the box.*

MOTHER: Please . . . oh, please, baby . . . jest a little bit o' greens, they's flavored with knuckles . . . oh, pussycat, please, you'll be alive again . . . that nigger can't stop you . . . pussycat . . .

BLACK MAN: (*stunned, staring, tears coming to his eyes. The* WOMAN *comes to comfort him*) What can I do. . . ?

BLACK WOMAN: Baby, baby . . .

BLACK MAN: My mother . . . and sister . . . crazy white things slobbering . . . God help me.

BLACK WOMAN: Oh, baby, you can't help it . . . you just can't help it.

MOTHER *and* SISTER *finally fall in the middle of the stage, holding each other, the* MOTHER *feeding the* SISTER, *with a spoon out of a small pot, some collard greens. The sister still sobs.*

SISTER: Ooooohhhhhhh God, God help me . . .

BLACK MAN: But this can't go, this stuff can't go. They'll die or help us, be black or white and dead. I'll save them or kill them. That's all. But not this shit . . . not this . . . horrible shit. (BLACK MAN *runs over and gets firehose, brings it back and turns it on* SISTER *and*

MOTHER) Now, let's start again, women. Let's start again. We'll see what you get . . . life . . . or death . . . we'll see . . .

He sprays them and they struggle until they fall out. Then the BLACK MAN *and* BLACK WOMAN *stand over the two on the floor.*

BLACK WOMAN: You think there's any chance for them? You really think so?

BLACK MAN: They're my flesh. I'll do what I can. (*Looks at her*) We'll both try. All of us, black people.

Curtain.

BOOKS OF RELATED INTEREST

Edgar White

REDEMPTION SONG And Other Plays

Redemption Song is a powerful blend of melodrama and ritual in which a poet returns to his island homeland to reclaim his birthright. *The Boot Dance,* set in an English mental hospital, deals forcefully with themes of exile, madness and revenge, while *Les Femmes Noires* probes the experiences of black women living in New York.

LAMENT FOR RASTAFARI And Other Plays

These plays offer a dark and disturbing picture of how blacks struggle to survive in a white society and with each other. *Lament for Rastafari* is part-ritual, part-panoramic vision of black/white relations within the confines of Rastafarian consciousness. *Like Them That Dream* concerns the violent conflict of conscience and the need for revenge when a black orderly discovers that he is expected to look after a dying member of the white South African secret police. *The Long and Cheerful Road to Slavery* consists of three one-act plays dealing with black relationships across time and geography.

'Highly recommended.' —*Time Out*

'Multiracial theatergoers . . . will appreciate Edgar White's straightforward and entertaining dramatization. His lightness of approach and the profundity of his statement are, I believe, the result of his clear and honest analysis of the post-colonial condition.'

—*Times Literary Supplement*

'Powerful and provocative.' —*Back Stage*

THE RISING: A Novel

Depicting a year in the life of a young boy, born and brought up on a small Caribbean island, Edgar White's novel describes a world of innocence, passion and brutality, and delineates the rituals of manhood and power that become so much a part of the growing boy's culture.

'Cuts to the core of the deep pull and profound claustrophobia of an insular community.' —*Kirkus Reviews*

'Edgar White has conveyed the drama of his story most beautifully in the players' speech, the music of which remains dominant.' —*The New Yorker*

'A strange and compelling energy on fine display here.'
—*The New York Times Book Review*

Edgar White is a poet, playwright and novelist. He was born on the Caribbean island Montserrat and lived in New York for many years. He now travels between London, New York and the Caribbean.

Roy Heath

'There is no longer any doubt that Heath is one of the world's best writers.' —*Kirkus Reviews*

KWAKU
or The Man Who Could Not Keep His Mouth Shut

This is the tale of Kwaku, who was reduced to a state of idiocy by intelligent men but made a spontaneous recovery. Part con-man, part Everyman, part Holy Fool, this picaresque saga follows Kwaku as he pursues his childhood dreams of wealth, happiness and position with a fanaticism that is only defeated by his own magnificent failings. Brilliantly conceived, deftly constructed and, above all, hugely enjoyable.

'A soldier Schweik in Civvy Street.'
—*Times Literary Supplement*

'A paradise of cartwheeling words and images.'
—*New Statesman*

'To be good, God knows, is enough to ask; to be astonishing into the bargain is a bonus.' —*The Guardian*

'Simply one of the most astonishingly good novelists of our time.' —*Edward Blishen*

'A beautiful writer.' —*Salman Rushdie*

'Rarely has the growth of a human mind been drawn so finely in fiction. Let other novelists read it and weep.'
—*The Philadelphia Inquirer*

'Cheering and riotous, it also keeps the heart-strings tugging.' —*The Observer*

'. . . wonderful comic set pieces that are Mr Heath's speciality.' —*The New York Times*

THE MINISTRY OF HOPE

Kwaku, Roy Heath's marvellous literary creation, is back; a small-time chiseller and ineffective healer in a village in Guyana but now down in the dumps: his wife has gone blind, his twin sons brutalize him, he is toppled from his perch as a healer and becomes once again the laughing stock of all and sundry. But fate intervenes, and Kwaku's fortunes are gradually resurrected — but only after barely escaping from a murderous mob does he finally succeed in establishing himself as a respected, wealthy citizen.

'A triumph . . . a wonderfully comic novel . . . A dramatic display of character in action that has seldom been matched by any contemporary novelist.'—*Kirkus Reviews*

'Heath's observation of the complexities of one man — his generosity and meanness, duty and forgetfulness, tenderness and cruelty — is wise and masterly.'
—*The Daily Telegraph*

'The reader accustomed to the rhythms of current popular fiction will find pleasure in the balanced phrasing, educated word choice and light alliteration of this author.' —*The Washington Times*

'Kwaku comes from a long line of literary buffoons who manage to triumph over the "intelligent" people around them. The language Mr Heath employs to describe this process is luxurious and densely baroque in places, sweetly comic in others.'—*The New York Times Book Review*

Roy Heath was born in British Guiana and came to England, at the age of 24, to become a lawyer and teacher. He is the winner of the Guardian Fiction Prize and was shortlisted for the Booker and Whitbread Prizes.

Sony Labou Tansi

'Central Africa's leading writer.' —*The New Yorker*

THE ANTIPEOPLE

A Novel

Translated by J.A. Underwood

As Principal of the North Lemba Teacher-Training College for Girls in Zaire, Dadou is a pillar of the community. Then an infatuated young student claims maliciously in a suicide note to have been made pregnant by him, and he becomes an outcast. He begins to neglect his work and takes to drink, his wife commits suicide, and his children are murdered by a vengeful mob. Dadou flees Zaire, only to become embroiled in the internecine power-struggle that plagues his refuge in the Congo. Having lost control of his destiny — and, almost his mind — Dadou becomes a terrorist whose life is a shattering saga of persecution and murder.

'One of the most prolific and original of the younger generation of writers to emerge from Francophone Africa in the post-Independence years.' —*The Guardian*

'His touch is deft and well-assured, and the translation wonderfully colloquial.' —*Kirkus Reviews*

'Through its urgent, sardonic narrative, *The Antipeople* brings us face to face with despair and death . . . and the constancy of love.' —*The New York Times Book Review*

'Tansi writes with urgent economy, blending a slangy bluntness with a Biblical lyricism, a lush sensuality, an insistent physicality of language.' —*The Village Voice*

Sony Labou Tansi was born in Kimwanza in the Congo in 1947 and for many years ran his own theater company in Brazzaville. He died in 1995. *The Antipeople* won the prestigious 'Grand Prix de l'Afrique Noire'.

Soleiman Fayyad

VOICES

A Novel

Translated from the Arabic with an introduction by Hosam Aboul-Ela

Hamid Ibn-Mustafa left the village of his birth at the age of ten and went to seek his fortune in Europe. Paris made him rich, and he is now a successful business man, married to an educated cosmopolitan French woman. But when he decides to visit his original family home in the eastern region of the Nile Delta, he unwittingly condemns both his wife and the village to become locked in a series of frustrating and disturbing encounters — cultural, religious and emotional — which are politely glossed over at first, until they finally become the makings of grim tragedy. *Voices* gives an objective but deeply compassionate glimpse of people's lives thrown into turmoil, in which the familiar and the strange continually press upon each other.

'Stunning . . . it rivals the fictions of Naguib Mahfouz in its psychological depth and sharp social commentary.'

—*Publishers Weekly*

'Intense and provocative . . . it deserves to be read.'

—*The Guardian*

'*Voices* works brilliantly.' —*The Independent*

'Crisply translated, *Voices* combines historical depth and psychological acuity within a taut, eventful narrative, bringing to life both its characters and the forces which drive them.' —*The Sunday Telegraph*

Soleiman Fayyad was born in 1929 and his first literary work was published in Cairo in 1961. Recognized as an exponent of contemporary Egyptian narrative — not unlike the Nobel prize-winner Naguib Mahfouz and Yusuf Idriss, the father of the modern Egyptian short story — Fayyad has become part of the generation of Egyptian writers to embrace a more uncompromising psychological fiction. *Voices* is his first work of fiction to be published in English.

Made in the USA
Columbia, SC
30 March 2019